A Guide to
# 25 FAVOURITE WATERFALLS
# IN THE
# LAKE DISTRICT

by
David Watson

First published in 2010 by
*Photoprint Scotland*

© David & Rosemary Watson
watson.dr@btinternet.com

ISBN 978-0-9559438-6-7

Photography by David & Rosemary Watson
Additional photographs of Stanley Force and Taylorgill
  by David Ross
Graphics and design by Rosemary Watson


Printed and bound by MLG, Glasgow

# CONTENTS

# INTRODUCTION

Man's interest in water is primeval. We are fascinated by it as children and we look for it on Mars as the first sign of life.

Spellbound!

Falling water is even more special. Myths and legends surround it, and poets have penned their verses about many Lakeland waterfalls. Sometimes its effect is almost spiritual and many of us are inspired by the awesome power of falling water.

In the Lake District, the word "force", from the Old Norse "fors" is often found, and simply means "waterfall".

## How Waterfalls are formed

Most Lake District waterfalls result from glaciation. During each glacial period, the main valleys, radiating from central Lakeland, were occupied by large glaciers, which effectively dammed the smaller tributary valleys coming in from the sides. As a result the main valleys were deepened to create the well-known "U" shape, and the tributary valleys were left "hanging" high up on the valley side. Often the hanging valley also had a corrie, now occupied by a tarn, which provides a small reservoir for the stream flowing from it.

Sour Milk Gill, on the south side of Buttermere, emerging from Bleaberry Tarn, is a fine example of a waterfall resulting from a hanging valley. (See Grid Ref NY165 155)

A similar example is Comb Beck which flows out from Burtness Comb, also into Buttermere.

Comb Beck cascading from Birtness Comb

4

Many falls also occur as a result of variations in the hardness of the rocks. In central Lakeland, in the area of the Borrowdale Volcanic Group of rocks, the constant variations of lavas, volcanic ash and other products of erupting volcanoes give rise to frequent changes in the hardness and resistance of rocks, creating constant variations in slope and the profile of stream beds.

In some cases, very hard intrusive rocks such as Dolerite have been injected into other, softer rocks, across a stream bed, forming a rock bar which is difficult to erode. A good example of this is on the Measand Beck on the north shore of Haweswater, (Grid Ref NY 485 155) in the last few hundred metres before it enters the lake. Waterfalls, or at least cascades, are also formed when the base level to which a stream is eroding is lowered, as with a change in sea-level, or the removal of a rock bar. The river then cuts down into its bed, and as it erodes backwards upstream, so the fall migrates headwards, leaving a gorge downstream, in front of the waterfall. This place on the stream is called a "nick point". Usually, however, such headward migration arrives, sooner or later, at a barrier of resistant rock, where perhaps there is already a waterfall. Nick point and waterfall coalesce and the cause of the falls becomes unclear. It is thought that falls on the river Lune at Tebay, just outside the National Park, occurred in this way.

SPOUT FORCE

## Types of Waterfalls

The form of each fall results largely from the inclination of the rock strata crossing the stream, in relation to the flow of the water. Most frequently the falls on a particular stream come in a variety of forms.

**Cataracts** are the most common and occur where water tumbles down a variable slope, with the stream-bed often strewn with boulders. Some cataracts occupy almost the whole length of a particular stream-bed, eg Sour Milk Ghyll, Buttermere.

Cataracts on Wyth Burn, Thirlmere

**Curtain and Ribbon falls** occur especially where the stream is crossed by horizontal rock strata, forming a narrow, unsupported, falling "ribbon" or "curtain" of water, depending on its width. Stanley Gill is a good example of this type of waterfall (see adjacent photograph).

**Spout**. A spout occurs when water is ejected outwards through a small gap in the rock (eg Spout Force featured on the previous page). Many Lakeland waterfalls are of this type, especially when swollen by heavy rain.

STANLEY GILL

## The Flora of Waterfalls

Few places in the lake District have what we might regard as strictly "natural" vegetation, that is except for inaccessible crags and crevices, deep gills and waterfalls. Only in these places do sheep have very limited access, and so it is there that a large variety of trees and smaller plants are able to survive and replenish. Elsewhere, a relatively impoverished vegetation, with a limited species range is found. The flora of waterfalls is best described by Mary Welsh in her series "A Naturalist's Guide to Lakeland Waterfalls throughout the year", books 1 to 4. In addition to frequently being inaccessible to foraging animals, waterfalls also tend to have their own special micro-climate, shady and the air full of moisture, giving rise to a highly distinctive range of plants.

On her walk to falls on Woundale Beck, she describes "Wood Sorrrel and liverwort ...in damper crevices and the leaves of butterwort, star shaped rosettes, cover the very wet areas."

Even the casual visitor, with no botanical knowledge whatsoever, cannot help but be aware of the abundance of tree species, as well as the dripping rocks clothed in a variety of mosses and ferns. The rocks around many falls never see direct sunlight and are permanently dripping with water.

Some common plants seen in damp, shady places

Coriolus Versicolor

Common Fern

Common Funnel Cap

Butterwort

Fly Agaric

Blackberry

Bluebell

Primrose

## Lakeland Waterfalls in literature and legend

The waterfalls of the Lake District were a magnet for the Romantic Poets, especially Wordsworth and Southey. In many ways they were responsible for the transformation of the image of the Lake District in the minds of the travelling public, from one of dark and oppressive woods and mountains, to a landscape of verdant beauty.

Southey wrote the famous poem for his children, which proved the "making" of the Lodore Falls. In it he explores every possible way of describing the water as it falls. The poem is very long, but this is a flavour.

> " How does the water
> Come down at Lodore?"
> My little boy asked me
> Thus, once on a time;
> And moreover he tasked me
> To tell him in rhyme..............
> From its sources which well
> In the tarn and the fell;
> From its fountains
> In the mountains......
> And guggling and struggling,
> And heaving and cleaving,
> And moaning and groaning;
> And glittering and frittering....
> And so, this way the water comes down
> at Lodore."

William Wordsworth wrote at least three poems about Aira Force, which he visited on numerous occasions. *The Somnambulist* (Sleepwalker) is the best known, and recounts the legend of a young girl, Emma, who sleep-walking, just as her lover was returning from battle, fell to her death over the falls. It begins...

> "List, ye who pass by Lyulph's Tower
> At eve; how softly then
> Doth Aira-force, that torrent hoarse,
> Speak from the woody glen!"

Lodore Falls

The poem describes the knight returning to his love, to find what he thought was a ghost, walking at the top of the falls. He then realised it was not a ghost, but Emma herself, and he leaned out to touch her.

> "...what followed who shall tell?
> The soft touch snapped the thread
> Of slumber - shrieking back she fell,
> And the stream whirled her down the dell
> Along its foaming bed........."

*The Somnambulist* was either inspired or written in 1833, and Aira Force has since become one of the "must do" visits in the Lake District, and certainly the most popular waterfall by far. If you only visit one, it must be Aira Force.

Waterfalls have been selected from most areas in the Lake District, and they have been sorted according to drainage basins, or valleys. With only a few exceptions we have chosen falls which are relatively easily accessible, with perhaps no more than 30 minutes walk from a car park. A few require almost no walking at all.

None of Lakeland's falls is very large, and a few which have been chosen are almost cameos of the genre. Many streams have delicate little falls which, to the picnicker and walker, are a sheer delight.

## Photographing Waterfalls

Once you've found your waterfall, the next thing is to photograph it. But this is often a little more tricky than you first might think. Here are a few guidelines, together with some of the scores of useful web-sites.

*www.digital-photography-school.com*
*www.outdoorphoto.com/guides*
*www.garyblack.com/waterfalls*

Firstly, choose a dull day, rather than a sunny day. Some suggest even choosing a rainy day, though this brings the risk of getting your camera wet. The author frequently photographs waterfalls from underneath an umbrella. Avoid sunny days if possible because of the massive amount of glare which occurs when falling water reflects sunlight.

Once you arrive at your waterfall, there are two major issues. Waterfalls, by their very nature, involve a mass of fast-moving, highly reflective water, and a background of the low light of a ravine or gorge. The correct light level for the background often leaves the water

overexposed, and vice-versa. The best advice is that you experiment, and always bracket shots around your chosen exposure.

Whatever the weather

The second issue is achieving the effect that you would like. There are really two possibilities, and a range between them. If you wish to "freeze" the action, then you need a wide aperture setting and a very fast shutter speed. However, if you wish to achieve a soft, artistic effect, then you need a very small aperture such as f22 and a slow shutter speed. The current vogue in photography is for the latter, but it is sensible to experiment with both approaches. If you use slow shutter speeds (maybe several seconds), you will certainly need to use a tripod. The best shots are generally taken looking upstream, towards the fall. Photos looking over the fall seldom seem to work. Another approach is to focus on only a small part of the fall, or even aspects of the rock or vegetation.

Small aperture, slow shutter speed

Large aperture, fast shutter speed

Our suggestion is to go and experiment. You will certainly make mistakes, but there is plenty of advice around.

Waders in the car may prove useful!

# HOW TO USE THIS BOOK

Simple Guides are designed to be used "hands on" and so the purpose of this book is to make it easy for you to visit each of 25 favourite waterfalls.

Each waterfall featured has a double page, which includes:
At least one photograph to give you a flavour of the falls.
A "how to get there" box, giving essential navigational information.
A Simple Map showing location, parking, paths and other useful information.

The Simple Maps in the book are essentially sketch-maps, based on data from Harvey's Lake District Outdoor Atlas, and are designed only for the purpose of navigating to each fall. For detail on surrounding areas, or for extending your walk, refer to Harvey's Outdoor Atlas or to the relevant Ordnance Survey sheet.

WARNING

Although waterfalls are delightful to visit, they are potentially dangerous places, with slippery rocks, steep cliffs, ravines and deep, fast-flowing water. Lakeland falls have been involved in many accidents over the years. Always treat waterfalls with respect. Especially keep children well-supervised at all times. Avoid bravado. Be careful with steep, unfenced drop-offs, which are very common in the gorge sections of waterfalls. This book encourages you to visit waterfalls, but your safety is your own responsibility.

## LEGEND

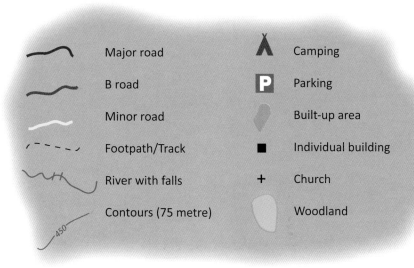

| | | |
|---|---|---|
| Major road | | Camping |
| B road | | Parking |
| Minor road | | Built-up area |
| Footpath/Track | | Individual building |
| River with falls | | Church |
| Contours (75 metre) | | Woodland |

450

## How to get there

Grid ref: NY 273 313
Located on Dash Beck, north of Skiddaw. Park at Peter House Farm (Grid ref NY 249 324), on the minor road east of Bassenthwaite village. Note there are two farm entrances. Park opposite the one furthest south. Round trip of about 6km (4 miles) Allow 1.5 to 2 hours. Easy walking. Whitewater Dash has the best-surfaced track leading to it of all the waterfalls in this book, a route which is part of the Cumbria Way. For 2 of the 3km, the track is the surfaced road to Dash Farm, and for the remaining kilometre, though not surfaced, it is in very good condition. If you are in a wheelchair, so long as you cope with the stiff slope of the first 400 metres, you can enjoy a lovely 3km trip at least to the foot of the falls.

WHITEWATER DASH

# WHITEWATER DASH
## BACK OF SKIDDAW

Whitewater Dash is one of the few falls in the Lake District which is visible from miles around. Indeed you get a good view even from the Castle Inn to Uldale road at grid ref NY 235 345. It is also one of a small number of falls not hidden away in a deep gill or ravine. The approach is across the open lower slopes of "Back of Skiddaw", with gorgeous views across the Dash Beck valley, and northwards towards the Solway Firth.

Open landscape on the approach to the falls

The falls are in a series of cascades, descending about 80 metres over several hundred metres and are best viewed from below, and indeed from several hundred metres away.
The Cumbria Way wends its way just to the south of the cascades, but then they become less visible as you get closer.

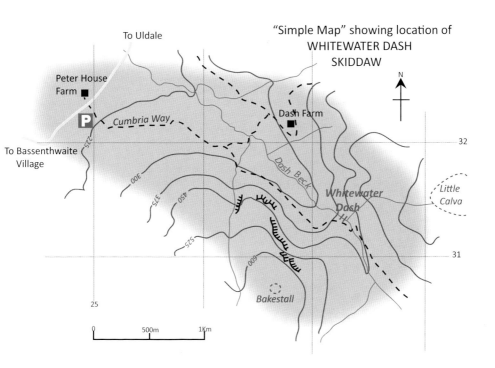

# THE HOWK IN WINTER

## How to get there
Grid Ref:  NY 319 397
Allow 30 minutes.
Located on Whelpo
Beck, just 400 metres
west of the Lakeland
village of Caldbeck,
close to the B5299.
There are various
short public rights of
way from the village,
none more than a
few hundred metres.
The author took the
route along the edge
of a grassy field from
Upton, southwest of
Caldbeck. Though
the access routes are
easy, paths around
the falls involve
steep steps and are
not wheelchair
friendly or suitable
for anyone with
walking difficulties.
However, the Howk
is possibly the best
fenced of all the
waterfalls visited,
and is therefore
more child-friendly
than most.

# THE HOWK
## CALDBECK

The Howk occurs at the head of a limestone gorge, where the Whelpo Beck squeezes through a gap of about one metre, and then ejects in a series of spouts, especially spectacular in spate. A footbridge crosses the beck right at the head of the falls, and a steeply stepped path winds along the northern bank, down to the ruined Howk Bobbin Mill.

The bobbin mill ran from 1857 to 1924, and in its day boasted the largest waterwheel in Britain, with a diameter of 42 feet 5 inches. Many Lake District waterfalls lent the power of their falling waters to various Industrial Revolution developments, and being fairly recent, this is one of the best preserved.

The village of Caldbeck is also well worth a visit, especially as it is the burial place of John Peel, who must be

The old bobbin mill

one of Lakeland's most famous sons. There is also the converted Priest's Mill, at the eastern end of the village, which has an excellent coffee-shop and some good craft shops.

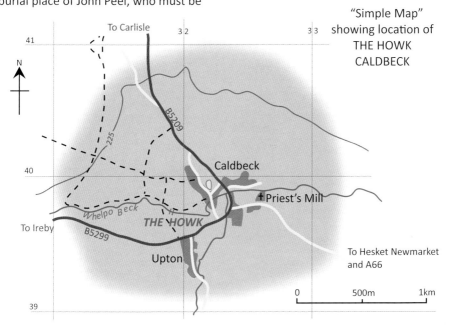
"Simple Map" showing location of THE HOWK CALDBECK

**How to get there**
Grid Ref: NX 265 187
Only 200 metres or so
Allow 30 minutes.
Located at the southeast
corner of Derwentwater,
on the Watendlath Beck,
behind the well-known
Lodore Hotel.
Approach via the B5289
to the Lodore Hotel from
either Keswick or
Borrowdale, or use one
the regular Keswick
launches across the lake.
If driving, park in the
hotel car park on the
west side of the road, for
which you have to pay at
reception. Walk along
the signed path around
the back of the hotel,
and the falls are less
than 200 metres away.
The path is not wheel-
chair friendly.

**LODORE FALLS**
in late May

# LODORE FALLS

The Lodore Falls are almost as iconic and perhaps as famous as Aira Force. They have featured in literature, especially the verses of poet Thomas Southey......

*" How does the water*
*Come down at Lodore?"*
*My little boy asked me*
*Thus, once on a time;*
*And moreover he tasked me*
*To tell him in rhyme.............*
*From its sources which well*
*In the tarn and the fell;*
*From its fountains*
*In the mountains......*
*And guggling and struggling,*
*And heaving and cleaving,*
*And moaning and groaning;*
*And glittering and frittering.....*
*And this way the water comes down at*
*Lodore"*

Extracts from "The Cataract of Lodore", Thomas Southey, 1774-1843

Though Lodore Falls have their own special charm, they are not especially spectacular, and because of the lack of easy parking, are perhaps much less visited than Aira Force.

As you approach, around the back of the Lodore Hotel, the building on the right houses a small hydro-electric station, which has been generating electricity for 100 years. Indeed the first powered tourist boat on Derwentwater was an electric-powered launch owned by the hotel and charged up daily by the hydro-electricity produced at the base of the falls.

The falls themselves are set in a

The Generator at Lodore

boulder-strewn ravine, as the Watend-lath Beck charges down to the lake, in various states of spate and spectacle, depending on the amount of recent rain. However, even in times of low water, the foot of the falls is a place of leafy trees and mosses, where visitors can find peaceful contemplation after only a little expenditure of energy.

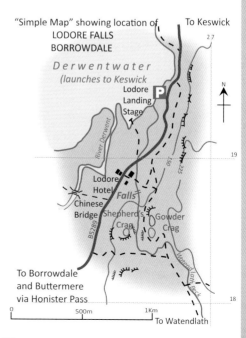
"Simple Map" showing location of LODORE FALLS BORROWDALE

17

## How to get there

Grid Ref: NY 230 123.

300 metres (about 1000 feet) of climbing to the top. Allow anything from 30mins to 2 hours.

Located on the western slopes of Seathwaite valley, opposite Seathwaite farm. Accessed from Borrowdale and the B5289 . Park on the verge north of Seathwaite Farm along with the usual scores of walkers. Turn right in the farmyard and head across the bridge over the Derwent. The falls are straight ahead, with a steep path just to the left, initially zig-zagging up the steep slope, and eventually on to Great Gable.

**SOUR MILK GILL**
from Seathwaite Farm

# SOUR MILK GILL
## SEATHWAITE

Sour Milk Gill, Seathwaite is one of three of the same name in the book. Especially when in spate, all exhibit variable amounts of foaming water, giving the impression of milk flowing down the mountain side.

The walk to Gillercombe, from which the beck flows, initially follows a well-worn zig-zag path just to the left of the gill, for this is one of Lakeland's most popular climbing routes. There are numerous cascades, mainly hidden in the trees, culminating in the final fall as Sour Milk Gill empties out of the corrie. Beyond here the path continues to Green Gable, Great Gable or down into Wasdale.

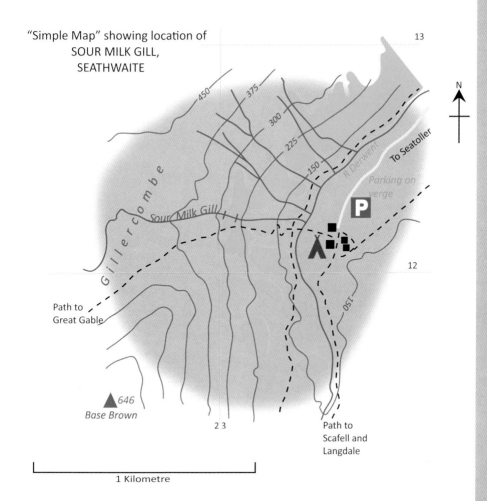

"Simple Map" showing location of SOUR MILK GILL, SEATHWAITE

**TAYLORGILL FORCE**

## How to get there

Grid Ref: NY 229 109. About 3km of a round trip which is sometimes rocky. Allow 1-1.5 hours. Not wheelchair friendly (or even very walker-friendly). Located at the southern end of Seathwaite valley, just over 1km (0.75 miles) south of Seathwaite farm. Seathwaite valley is south of Borrowdale, accessed via the B5289 from either Keswick or Buttermere. Park along with all the other walkers north of Seathwaite farm. It may be very busy, with literally hundreds of vehicles.

In the farmyard, opposite the coffee shop, turn right through an archway in the farm buildlings, and follow the path which soon crosses the embryonic River Derwent. Over the bridge one path zig-zags up beside Sour Milk Gill, which is immediately in front of you. Take the other path, which turns left along the banks of the Derwent.

Initially the path is very poor and rocky, and you generally have to find your own way through the boulder field along the bottom of Fawn Crag. After about 500 metres it turns right, goes diagonally uphill, and continues until Taylorgill Force comes into view.

# TAYLORGILL FORCE

Taylorgill Force, at about 30 metres (100 feet) is the highest single fall in Borrowdale. It is contained within a narrow, wooded ravine. During dry times the Force is series of cascades, but in times of heavy rain, which are frequent in England's wettest place, it becomes a single, impressive cascade, as in the photograph. Unusually, Taylorgill Force does not have the plunge pool associated with many falls. Instead, the base of the fall is littered with the boulders hurled over the fall during the many times of flood.

"Simple Map" showing location of
TAYLORGILL FORCE

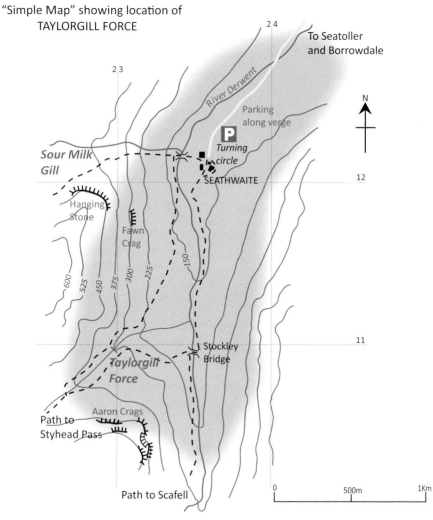

21

## How to get there

Grid Ref: NY 400 205
Various routes and times. Allow 1-2 hours. A stiff little climb which is not wheel-chair or push-chair friendly. Located on the Aira Beck, accessed either off the A592 Penrith-Ullswater road, or the A5091, which runs north from Ullswater, west of the Aira Force car park.

The main access point is at the clearly signed National Trust car park, Grid Ref: NY 401 201, where there is interpretive information. A series of paths leads up both sides of the beck. Most visitors turn round at the main fall, but the path continues up the beck, first to High Force, then the "Chasm" and the "Cascades", and eventually to Dockray. An alternative access is from either the National Trust car park at NY 398 205 0n the A5091 road, or the layby further up the road. Paths from here lead to the various upper falls.

# AIRA FORCE AND AIRA BECK WATERFALLS

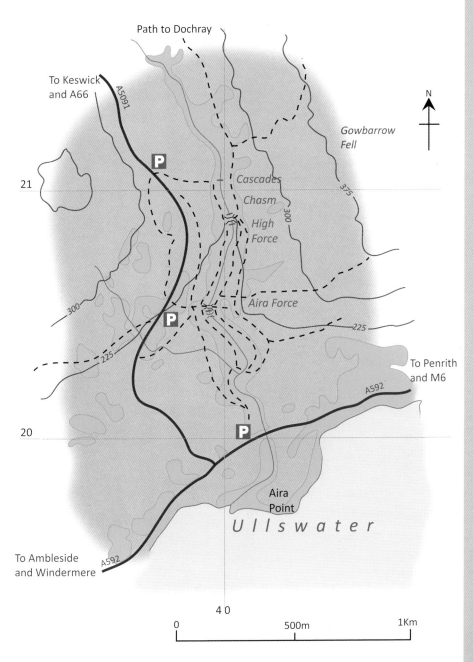

Path to Dochray

To Keswick
and A66

A5091

Gowbarrow
Fell

N

21

375

Cascades

Chasm

300

High
Force

Aira Force

300

225

P

225

To Penrith
and M6

A592

20

P

Aira
Point

*U l l s w a t e r*

To Ambleside
and Windermere

A592

4 0

| 0 | 500m | 1Km |

Above the falls is a sequence of even prettier cascades, water-spouts and chasms, extending along the beck towards the village of Dochray. The Cascades, about 500 metres above the main fall, are especially attractive.

WARNING
As with all waterfalls, Aira Force is potentially dangerous, with an unprotected, sheer drop in places. Children should be supervised at all times.

Aira Force is Lakeland's most visited waterfall, with a host of further cascades and water-spouts further up the Aira Beck, beyond the main fall. The falls have been a popular visitor attraction for over 200 years, and inspired at least three Wordsworth poems, the most famous being *The Somnambulist (Sleepwalker)*, about a young girl who, sleep-walking, tragically fell to her death over the falls.

> *"......how softly then*
> *Doth Aira-force, that torrent hoarse,*
> *Speak from the woody glen!*
> *Fit music for a solemn vale!*
> *And holier seems the ground*
> *To him who catches on the gale*
> *The spirit of a mournful tale,*
> *Embodied in the sound....."*

Aira Force is set in a beautiful woodland park, planted by the Howard family in the late 18th and early and mid-19th centuries. In 1906 the falls and the area around were bought by the National Trust.

Part of the woodland park

The main falls are spectacular, as they cascade 70 feet between two bridges. The best views are undoubtedly obtained from the lower bridge, as shown on page 22.

Aira Beck has numerous bridges between the National Trust car park and Dochray, the most northerly being just above High Force.

The approach to the bridge above High Force

Many visitors combine a waterfalls visit with a more extended walk, either continuing up the beck to Dockray or ascending Gowbarrow Fell.

A glimpse of Ullswater from the path

**SCALEHOW FORCE**
**in December**

### How to get there

Grid Ref: NY 403 188

This is the easy route. For other ways of getting there, see main text.

Take the minor road from Pooley Bridge at the northern end of Ullswater which is signposted for Martindale. Continue as far as Sandwick, keeping right at St Peter's Church. Park along the verge before Sandwick or in the hamlet itself.

Take the path west to Patterdale, which starts just before Sandwick. After about 0.5 km, immediately after an isolated barn, cross over a stream, and head diagonally uphill on a grassy path for about 400 metres, and the main fall becomes visible.

Return by the same route. Only 3km round trip (about 2 miles). Easy walking. Allow 1-1.5 hours.

"Simple Map" showing location of
SCALEHOW FORCE

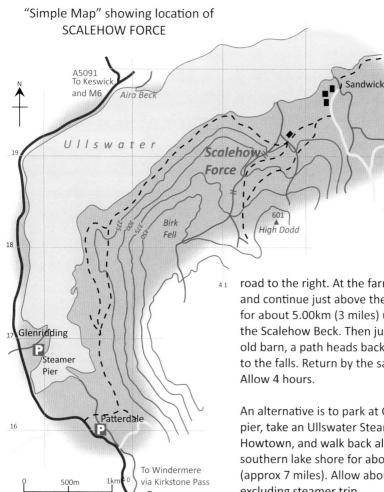

road to the right. At the farm, turn left, and continue just above the lake shore for about 5.00km (3 miles) until you cross the Scalehow Beck. Then just before an old barn, a path heads back up hill, close to the falls. Return by the same route. Allow 4 hours.

An alternative is to park at Glenridding pier, take an Ullswater Steamer to Howtown, and walk back along the southern lake shore for about 11.5 km (approx 7 miles). Allow about 4 hours, excluding steamer trip.

For whichever route, Scalehow falls are approached across open, bracken-covered fell. They occur as the beck slides over a smooth rock buttress, falling about 30 metres (100 feet). After another few hundred metres you arrive at the upper falls, an attractive curtain fall.

The hard route, about 13.00 km (approx 8 miles), is often very rocky and involves numerous short but stiff climbs.
Park at Patterdale Hotel (pay and display) Walk 100 metres along the main road towards Glenridding and take the farm

**How to get there**

Grid Ref: NY 314 137
Located on the western side of Thirlmere only about 500 metres from the road. Allow 45 minutes to 1 hour for the round trip.

Park at Grid Ref: NY 315 140 (also has toilets) and follow the zig-zag path which goes fairly steeply uphill. For the last 100 metres, until it levels out at the lower falls, the path is more of a rock "staircase".

Not wheelchair friendly.

DOB GILL
lower fall

# DOB GILL

Dob Gill falls are on the beck which drains Harrop Tarn. The path from the car park winds upwards through mixed woodland, mainly of conifers and beech. When the author visited in autumn, beech leaves almost obscured the route. The falls are quite delightful and fully justify the stiff little climb to get there. The path arrives initially at the lower fall, shown in the photo, and then continues to Harrop Tarn via the impressive upper cascade.

"Simple Map" showing location of
DOB GILL,
THIRLMERE

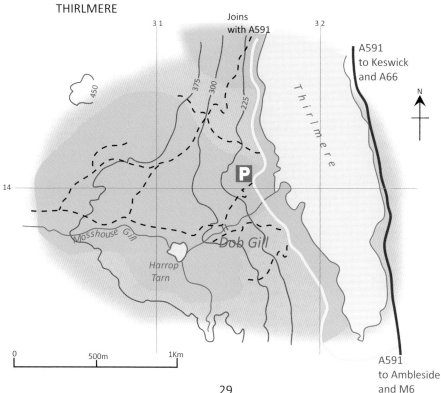

Joins with A591

A591 to Keswick and A66

Thirlmere

N

450

375  300

225

P

14

Mosshouse Gill

Dob Gill

Harrop Tarn

0       500m       1Km

A591 to Ambleside and M6

29

**How to get there**

Grid ref: NY328 125

30 minutes round trip

Located on the northern side of Dunmail raise, east of the A591. This is probably the easiest to access of all the Thirlmere waterfalls. It is located east of the main road, just beyond the southern edge of the forest and is visible from the road. There are various car-parking options, either at Steel End or next to the Wyth Burn church. It is also possible to park safely at the start of the forest road without blocking the entrance. (Grid ref: NY 325 128) There is a gentle walk of about 400 metres up the forest track, and there are stiles if the gates are closed. At the edge of the forest, a footpath with two wooden bridges crosses the beck at the base of the falls.

**BIRKSIDE GILL**
in November

# BIRKSIDE GILL

This is a splendid waterfall, especially in times of spate. There are two major falls, joined by a series of cataracts, all of which is visible from the bottom. The beck divides below the falls and the streams pass under two solid wooden bridges, which provide "viewing platforms". Being so accessible, this makes a lovely location for a picnic on fine summer days.

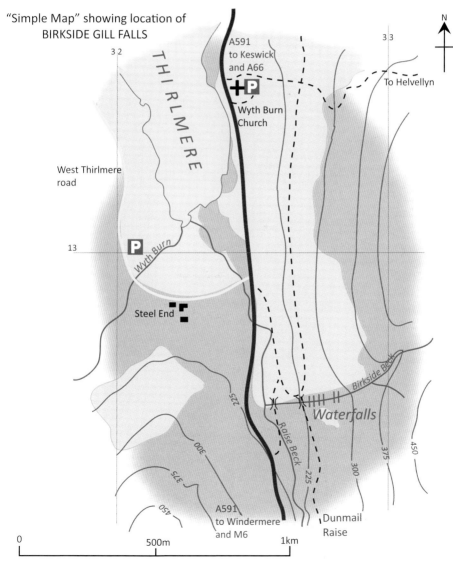

"Simple Map" showing location of
BIRKSIDE GILL FALLS

N

3 2

A591
to Keswick
and A66

3 3

✛ P

To Helvellyn

Wyth Burn
Church

West Thirlmere
road

T H I R L M E R E

13

P  Wyth Burn

Steel End

Birkside Beck

225

Waterfalls

Raise Beck

300

225

375

450

300

225

300

375

450

A591
to Windermere
and M6

Dunmail
Raise

0          500m          1km

## How to get there

Grid Ref: NX 182 260
Located on the Aiken Beck, a stream on the western side of Whinlatter Forest Park, and only about 400 metres from Scawgill Bridge, on the Lorton to Braithwaite road. Although there is a Forestry Commission car park, the path through the forest to the falls is somewhat overgrown as it passes through an area of clear-fell.

By far the easiest route is to park at Scawgill Bridge on the western side of Whinlatter Pass (Grid Ref: NX 177 257), where there is space for about three cars, and to take the path along the western side of the Aiken Beck, about 400 metres to the falls. The path is easy, with a little climb at the finish to a small viewing area. A short scramble down to the beck gives access to the base of the falls. Not wheelchair friendly, but baby buggies could cope with the first 200 metres.

**SPOUT FORCE**

# SPOUT FORCE
## WHINLATTER

The key to the existence of Spout Force can be seen in the abandoned slate quarry at Scawgill Bridge. The band of resistant rock extends north-eastwards until it crosses the line of the Aiken Beck, causing the natural step which produces Spout Force.

The view of the falls and the rock outcrop from the viewing area illustrates the origins of the waterfall. In times of low water it is possible to approach from below in order to obtain a more complete view, though there is no formal path in this area.

The way to the falls, along the first 100 metres of the Aiken Beck provides a nice picnic spot, especially if you prefer to be away from the hurly-burly of the Whinlatter Visitor Centre along the road, but still need to be near your car.

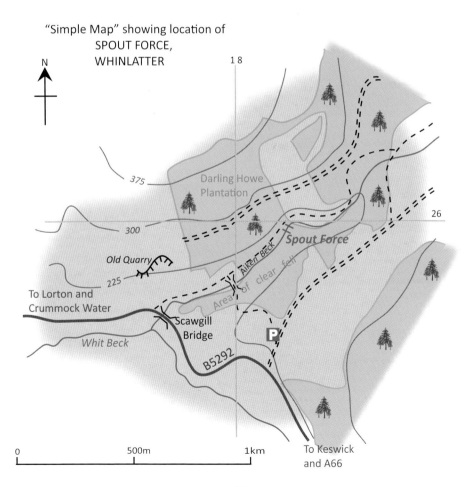

"Simple Map" showing location of SPOUT FORCE, WHINLATTER

N

18

375

Darling Howe Plantation

300

26

Old Quarry

Aiken Beck

Spout Force

225

Area of clear fell

To Lorton and Crummock Water

Scawgill Bridge

P

Whit Beck

B5292

0      500m      1km

To Keswick and A66

### How to get there

Grid Ref: NX 193 175
Approximately 200 metres to waterfalls. Allow 20-30 minutes. Located at the head of Newlands Pass. The series of cascades is in the area called "Newlands Hause". Easy access, although it is not wheelchair friendly.
Situated on the minor road which starts from the west at the church in Buttermere, and from the east via Braithwaite village and Newlands valley and Keskadale. Right at the top of the pass is a car park, from which the waterfalls are visible, only 100 to 200 metres away. There is a short, fairly level, easy walk which takes only a few minutes.

**MOSS FORCE**

# MOSS FORCE

Moss Force is the Lake District's most accessible large waterfall. The Force is made up of a series of several cascades, over several hundred metres, and a path from the car park at the top of the pass makes it possible to visit the falls in only a few minutes. The path forks, the left route going to a little pool at the foot of the falls, and the right fork approaching the base of the upper cascade. As with most Lakeland waterfalls, Moss Force can vary from a spectacular, sometimes icy torrent to a series of gentle trickles.

Moss Force

Spectacular view from the waterfalls

"Simple Map" showing location of
MOSS FORCE

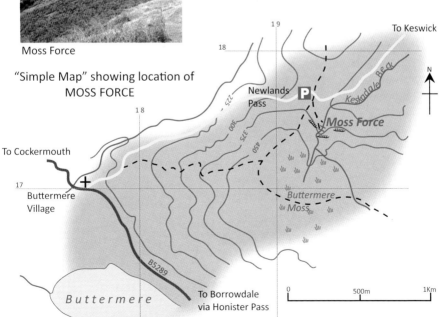

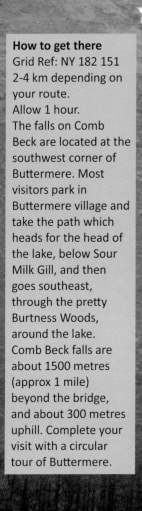

## How to get there

Grid Ref: NY 182 151
2-4 km depending on
your route.
Allow 1 hour.
The falls on Comb
Beck are located at the
southwest corner of
Buttermere. Most
visitors park in
Buttermere village and
take the path which
heads for the head of
the lake, below Sour
Milk Gill, and then
goes southeast,
through the pretty
Burtness Woods,
around the lake.
Comb Beck falls are
about 1500 metres
(approx 1 mile)
beyond the bridge,
and about 300 metres
uphill. Complete your
visit with a circular
tour of Buttermere.

**COMB BECK**
on a rainy November day

# COMB BECK

When visiting Comb Beck, it is also possible to park southeast of the lake off the B5289 Honister Pass road at Gatesgarth, (pay and display). Cross the road and take the path which heads around the lake in a clockwise direction. The walk to the falls is about 1km, and the falls will be on your left. Allow a minimum of 1 hour.

As with Sour Milk Gill, Comb Beck emerges from a corrie, in this case Burtness (or Birkness) Comb, before cascading downhill. Except in times of spate, as in the photo, the falls are considerably less threatening than their more famous neighbour, and it is possible to explore them in much greater safety. Unusually, at various places, and depending on the amount of water, the beck divides, as it diverts around rock islands.

If you are on a "round Buttermere" walk, Comb Beck falls make an ideal place to stop off for a picnic, especially with children.

The photograph opposite was taken in heavy rain at the time of the record-breaking floods of autumn 2009.

"Simple Map" showing location of COMB BECK FALLS, BUTTERMERE

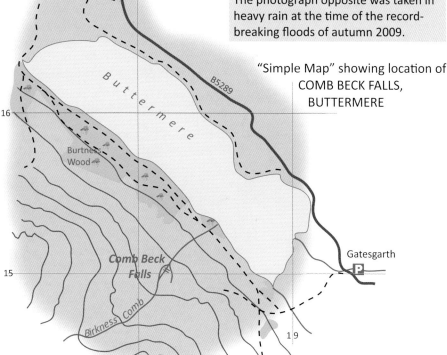

37

## How to get there

Grid Ref: NY 151 172
About 10 km (6 miles) round trip. Allow 2-3 hrs.
Park in the car park at Buttermere village (Grid Ref: NY 175 169) on the B5289 road which runs from Cockermouth past Crummock Water and Buttermere, over Honister Pass into Borrowdale. Or approach from Keswick over Newlands Pass.

Walk around the Fish Hotel and head across the valley between the lakes, keeping right at the first path junction. After crossing a pretty bridge, turn right, through the woods, on to a path of variable quality. At the end of the woods, take the path diagonally uphill to the left. The path is fairly erratic, sometimes difficult to see, and is often very rocky, as it skirts the edge of a boulder field. Eventually the path becomes more obvious, and after passing through a wall, descends the final few metres to a wooden bridge, with the falls just upstream. Return by the same route.

**SCALE FORCE**
hidden deep in a ravine

# SCALE FORCE

Scale Force is Lakeland's tallest water-fall, with a single drop of about 40 metres (about 120 feet). During Victorian times, it became one of the "must see" locations in the Lake District, and a procession of visitors would make the trek across from Buttermere, having been driven over Newlands Pass from Keswick. The main cascade is almost concealed in a deep cleft in the rock, and as with many waterfalls in the Lake District, Scale Force remains hidden until you arrive just below. It is possible to scramble almost to the base, where there is a pretty cascade about 6 metres high, with the main fall a narrow stream of water, hidden in the trees behind. Wordsworth, a keen visitor of waterfalls described "..a fine chasm, with a lofty, though but slender fall of water."

View from Scale Force over Crummock Water

A visit to Scale Force offers some fine views over Crummock Water and along Buttermere valley. In addition, Sour Milk Gill, quite spectacular during periods of heavy rain, flows into the northwest end of Buttermere, and many waterfall watchers combine this fall with their trip to Scale Force.

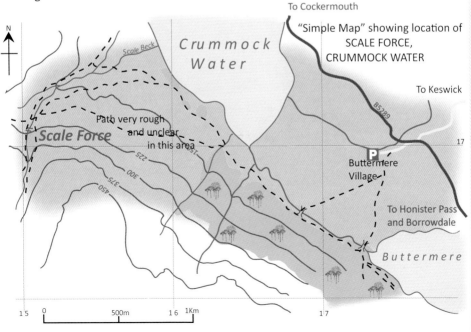

39

Do not be tempted to climb up the face of Sour Milk Gill, or you may join the numerous others who have died doing the same. The path to the south was deliberately diverted to avoids the falls, because of the danger (and the temptation).

SOUR MILK GILL,
Buttermere

# SOUR MILK GILL, BUTTERMERE

Sour Milk Gill is one of several cascades of the same name in the Lake District. All of them in spate after the frequent heavy rains give the impression of a torrent of milk, roaring down the mountain side. If you wish to truly experience Sour Milk Gill is its glory, be there after the rains. At other times the falls may be a mere trickle.

This is one of the many falls resulting from a "hanging valley" produced by the over-deepening of the main valley relative to the tributary valley during glaciation. The corrie occupied by Bleaberry Tarn literally "hangs" 300+ metres (1000 feet) above Buttermere valley, resulting in a spectacular cascade for the stream leaving the tarn.

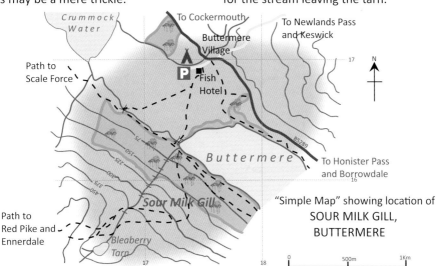

"Simple Map" showing location of
SOUR MILK GILL,
BUTTERMERE

## How to get there

Grid Ref: From NX 166 156 to NX 173 163. A series of cascades, over 400 metres or so from Bleaberry Tarn to the north-western corner of Buttermere.

From nearest car parking the walk is less than 1km (just over 0.5 miles) to base of the falls. Allow 30 minutes round trip. Wheelchair possible, though bumpy. Visible (and sometimes audible) from across the valley, where you can view the whole of Sour Milk Gill, especially during a time of spate. However, to get to the foot of the falls, park in the National Park car park in Buttermere village (off the B5289). Walking from the car park, turn right around the Fish Hotel and follow the path. When the path forks, keep left and head directly across the valley bottom to the foot of the falls and the bridge across the Scale Beck.

If you wish to view the falls from the top, take the path to the southeast via Burtness Wood. The west end of Butter-mere is a good picnic spot.

### How to get there
Grid Ref: NY 119 214. 2-2.5 km. Allow 1 hour.
Located on the western side of Loweswater,
conveniently next to a forest track.
Park north of the lake at Grid Ref NY 119 224
and proceed north. You can take the path
which heads left into the field and across the
marsh at the end of the lake on "duck-
boards". However, on a visit in November,
we discovered that the "duck-boards" did
not quite reach the edge of the marsh, with
rather wet and muddy consequences, so
maybe better to go along the road and turn
left into the road beyond Waterend.
Continue to Hudson Place farm at the top of
the hill, and then left on the rough track for
"Holme Wood". Go through the gate into the
National Trust-owned woodland, and after
about 400 metres take the first forest track
to the right. The falls are 400-500 metres
uphill, with a bridge as a viewing point.

**HOLME FORCE**
from the forestry track

# HOLME FORCE

This is one of the quieter nooks of the Lake District, and in comparison with many other falls, you will find few visitors sharing this lovely little walk. The route to the falls passes through beautiful mixed woodland, with many varieties of trees, including oak, ash, beech and birch, together with holly and some magnificent conifers.

In early publications writers refer to Holme Force's twin falls, about 4 metres apart. During our visit, in spite of heavy rain, the lower falls had only one main cascade, with the former "twin" now blocked off.

However, this easy-to-access fall is still spectacular, with a series of cascades and spouts above the main fall.

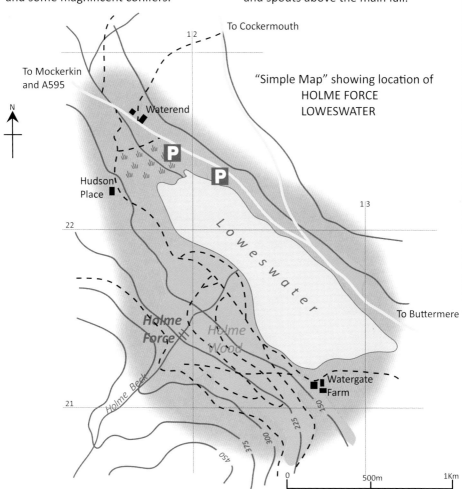

"Simple Map" showing location of
HOLME FORCE
LOWESWATER

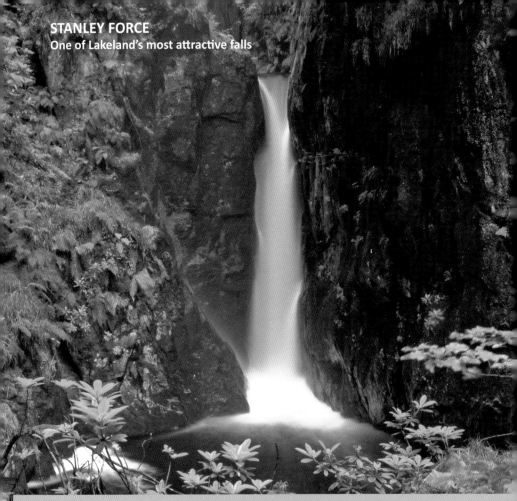

## STANLEY FORCE
One of Lakeland's most attractive falls

**How to get there**

Grid ref: SD 175 995

Arrive either by road or by rail. By road the route goes through Eskdale towards Hardknott Pass, with parking either at Dalegarth Station (SD 173 007) or at the National Trust car park, 500 metres to the south.

By rail take the Ravenglass-Eskdale narrow gauge railway to its terminus at Dalegarth. On leaving the station turn right. After a few hundred metres turn left on a minor road which, after crossing the River Esk, leads to the National Trust car park. After the surfaced road becomes a track, turn left on to the path marked "Stanley Ghyll, Birker Moor and Waterfall". Crossing the stream, follow the left bank for about 1 kilometre, after which there are three wooden bridges, first leading to the right bank, then back to the left bank. Then, just below the falls, by which time Stanley Ghyll is a narrow ravine, cross again to the right bank, where there is a safe viewing point. Return by the same route or, alternatively, cross over the third bridge, and turn left uphill. This route quickly takes you to a path junction where the route to the right takes you to the National Trust car park below.

However, if you continue for almost another kilometre, you can cross Stanley Ghyll to the right bank, and then turn back downhill towards either the National Trust car park or Dalegarth Station.

# STANLEY FORCE

Stanley Force is rightly regarded as one of the Lake District's prettiest waterfalls. As with many falls it is located in a deep ravine, lush with the luxuriant vegetation originally widespread, but now only found in areas protected from the teeth of sheep. There are differences amongst commentators as to its height of the falls. Suffice to say that there is a series of cascades and pools, the most spectacular of which falls as a beautiful narrow curtain fall, emptying into a pool at the bottom of a 45 metre-deep tree-framed ravine. David Ross, on the Britain Express website, describes Stanley Force in summer as "almost tropical".

With Stanley Force being at the Dalegarth end of the Ravenglass-Eskdale railway, an excursion to the falls can form part of a lovely day out. By car it can also take in the spectacular Hardknott and Wrynose Passes, linking Langdale and Ambleside with the western Lake District.

If you wish to use an alternative return route, we suggest you refer either to Harvey Lake District Outdoor Atlas or OS Landranger map sheets 89 and 96.

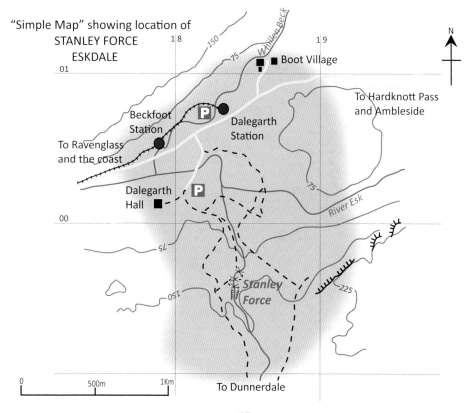

"Simple Map" showing location of STANLEY FORCE ESKDALE

45

# TARN BECK PITCHERS

**How to get there**

Grid Ref: SD 229 963 and for a few hundred metres northwards. Adjacent to the road.

Leave the main A595 South Lakes road at Duddon Bridge, west of Broughton in Furness, and head north on the minor road, first to Ulpha and then to Seathwaite. The cataracts are on the Tarn Beck just beyond the church. There are numerous little places to park.

# TARN BECK PITCHERS
## (SEATHWAITE CATARACTS)

The name "pitchers" was given to us in the Newfield Inn, Seathwaite, as the authentic local name, though we can find no other mention in the waterfall literature.

The Pitchers do not have the threat of many of the waterfalls we include, either in water volume or in their fall, so they are much more suitable for children.

Our photographs were taken under an umbrella, in the pouring rain on a November day when many Lakeland roads were flooded, so the amount of water was unusual.

On summer days the Pitchers often become a series of gentle little cascades, suitable for paddling, and the woodland areas next to the parking spots are nice for family picnics.

The Newfield Inn is most welcoming, either for a drink or a meal

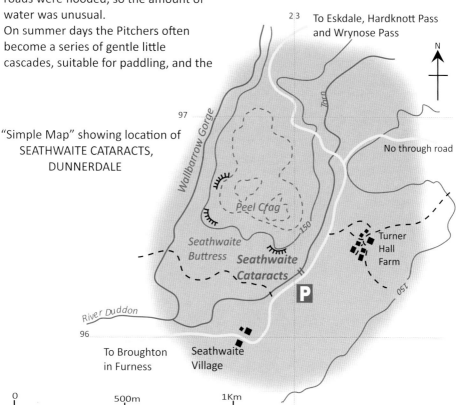

"Simple Map" showing location of SEATHWAITE CATARACTS, DUNNERDALE

**SOUR MILK GILL
GRASMERE**
Taken in autumn

## How to get there

Grid Ref: NY 318 087.  4km round trip. Allow 1-1.5 hours.

Located on the Easedale Beck as it flows from Easedale Tarn towards Grasmere. Park in one of several car-parks in Grasmere, and take the Easedale road, which runs northwest out of the village. At Grid Ref: NY 331 082 a well-worn path leaves the road across two slate bridges over the beck and heads towards the falls visible in the distance. During the author's visit parts of this much-used path were truly awful, and in desperate need of repair.

As you get near to the base of the falls, an old, now unused track between two walls moves off to the right. After 100 metres this leads to a little grassy area beside the beck, from which our photo was taken, and a nice place to picnic.

# SOUR MILK GILL
## GRASMERE

Sour Milk Gill, Grasmere is one of three waterfalls of the same name which we include, all given their title because of the milk-like effect they have when in spate. Being on a massively popular walking route, and close to the Lakeland "Mecca" of Grasmere, these falls are much visited. The falls are not hidden away in a deep ravine, but can be seen from far away, even from the main road at the foot of Dunmail Raise.

It is a pity the access path is in such a poor state as the falls can be truly spectacular.

Not wheel chair or baby buggy friendly!

"Simple Map" showing location of
**SOUR MILK GILL**
**GRASMERE**

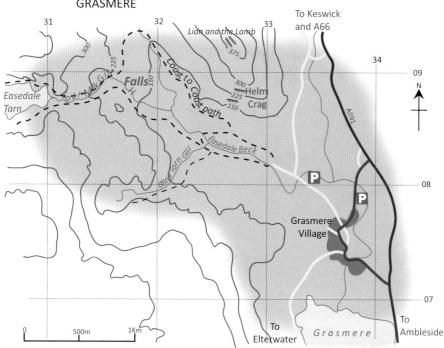

**How to get there**

Grid Ref: NY 365 067

Park beside Rydal Church on the road up to Rydal Mount, just off the A591 Ambleside to Grasmere road. This may be very busy at times, as most cars will be of visitors to Wordsworth's final home. Walk up hill for 200-300 metres, following the tarmac, then concrete road, which then becomes a track. Continue with the wall on your right, past the campsite and the Garden Cottage until you reach a gate, at which point the path to the falls heads through a gap in the wall into the woods, in the grounds of Rydal Hall. Follow the path through a conifer plantation, through a gate and along a fence to the beck. A rather rickety bridge gives access to a path on the left bank, which winds up to the falls.

HIGH FALL, RYDAL,
in summer spate

# HIGH FALL, RYDAL

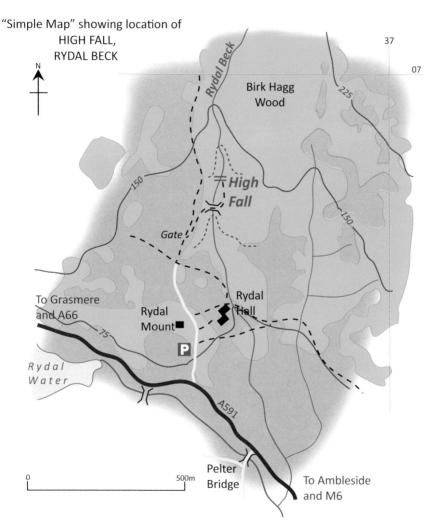

"Simple Map" showing location of HIGH FALL, RYDAL BECK

N

Rydal Beck

Birk Hagg Wood

37

07

225

150

High Fall

150

Gate

To Grasmere and A66

Rydal Mount

Rydal Hall

P

75

Rydal Water

A591

0      500m

Pelter Bridge

To Ambleside and M6

The beck was in spate during the author's visit, and the deeply incised valley was filled with a thunderous roar. A series of splendid cascades starts just above the bridge, which is situated at an abandoned weir. Follow the beck upstream 100 metres or so to High Fall, which descends from the top of the gorge into a deep plunge pool. In flood the series of falls and cascades on the Rydal beck is an impressive sight, and because it is contained within a narrow valley, the noise of the water leaves one in no doubt as to its power.

**How to get there**
Grid Ref NX 385 045.
On Stockghyll, the
beck which flows
into the centre of
Ambleside from the
east. Less than 1 km
(0.5 miles) depend-
ing on starting point.
Allow 1 hour.
From the town, take
the road on the right
side of Barclays Bank
in the centre of
Ambleside. Continue
until a sign indicat-
ing the falls and the
woodland park to
the left. The falls are
a further few
hundred metres.
Alternatively, you
can drive to a small
parking area (only 4
or 5 cars), at the
entrance to the
woodland park. The
path is relatively
easy, except for a
little climb in the last
200 metres. Wheel-
chair friendly from
the very top of the
road.

**STOCKGHYLL FORCE**
in summer

# STOCKGHYLL FORCE

This is the only waterfall in the Lake District which can be easily accessed from the centre of a town. The falls are located in a shady, mossy woodland park on the eastern edge of Ambleside. Lots of park benches (though many, sadly in a poor state of maintenance) testify to the walk to the falls originally being a much more popular activity in the past than it is today, which is a shame, as they are so easily accessible. Stockghyll is full of little cascades, and at the falls themselves, the stream is split into two, producing a spectacular "Y"-shape, with a fall of approximately 22 metres (about 70 feet). There are handy viewing locations along the protective fence, and a bridge over the top of the falls.

"Simple Map" showing location of STOCKGHYLL FORCE

A591
to Coniston

N

225
150
75

Kirkstone Pass

05

P
Stockghyll
Waterfall

P
AMBLESIDE

04

593
o Coniston

P

75
150

03

*WINDERMERE*

A591
to Windermere

0    500m    1Km

3 8

Stockghyll and its fall from Wansfell contributed much to the origins of Ambleside. At least 12 different mills were powered by the falling water, producing a range of goods such as bobbins, fabrics and corn, the earliest records of mills dating from around the 14th century. Though all of them are now closed, evidence of former mills along the beck remains in the form of abandoned weirs and converted mill buildings.

Old weir on Stockghyll

**How to get there**
Grid Ref: NY 327 032
400 metre walk.
Allow 30 minutes.
Park in the small layby on the south side of Colwith Bridge (Grid Ref NY 330 031), just off the main Ambleside to Coniston road. There are two stiles leading to the Colwith Falls path, both near the bridge. The path then winds through delightful woods for about 300m passing a series of small cascades on the way.
Not wheelchair friendly.

COLWITH FORCE IN SPATE

# COLWITH FORCE

Colwith Falls is one of the easiest waterfalls to access, and although not wheelchair friendly, involves only a short walk from the bridge through National Trust property. A rock bar extends across the course of the River Brathay, causing it to divide into a several "fingers". The photograph was taken during a November spate and the sight was spectacular and noisy. However, the falls produce a fine spectacle at almost any time of year, a reliability which, in former times, resulted in a small hydro-electric scheme using the vertical drop created by the fall. Electricity is no longer produced here, but the small stone-built generator house remains at the foot of the falls.

Generator house downstream from the falls

"Simple Map" showing location of
COLWITH FORCE
AND
SKELWITH FORCE

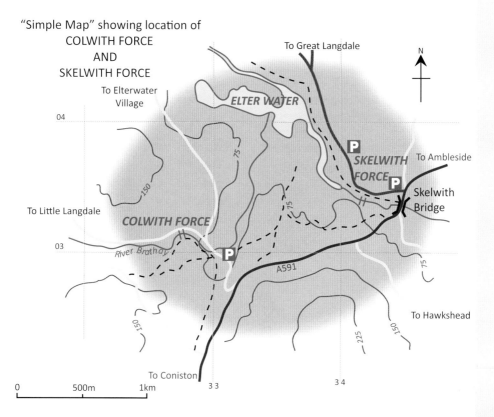

To Great Langdale

N

To Elterwater
Village

ELTER WATER

04

SKELWITH
FORCE

To Ambleside

Skelwith
Bridge

To Little Langdale

COLWITH FORCE

03

River Brathay

A591

To Hawkshead

To Coniston

| 0 | 500m | 1km |

3 3

3 4

55

**SKELWITH FORCE**
in summer spate

**How to get there**
Grid Ref: NY342 035
200 metre walk.
Five minutes to the falls.
One of the easiest to
access of all the waterfalls
in this book. Park along
the roadside at the start
of the B5343 road to
Great Langdale just after
it leaves the main
Ambleside-Coniston road.
Proceed first along the
road, and then along the
riverside path for about
200 metres.

# SKELWITH FORCE

Skelwith Force lies on the River Brathay just upstream from Skelwith Bridge, where the river drops over a final step from the volcanic rocks of central Lakeland to the softer Silurian rocks of the south, almost to the level of Windermere. Because the River Brathay drains Great and Little Langdale, at times of spate, such as when our photographs were taken, it can be spectacular and noisy.

As long ago as 1830, Jonathan Otley wrote:

*"Skelwith Force ..has the most copious supply of water of any cascade among the lakes".*

During the author's visit, with heavy rain and high water, it seemed that the falls become potentially dangerous. A pair of little access bridges invite exploration onto slippery rocks next to the roaring torrent. Bravado seemed the most likely motivation for most of the visitors who were tempted close to the edge of the water. Certainly not suitable for unsupervised children (or adults!)

Otley suggests that the best view is from the south and west side, with the Langdales in the background, though this is difficult to achieve.

For directions, please refer to the map on page 55.

Skelwith Bridge

**How to get there**
Grid Ref: SD 308 988. This is the only waterfall we list which can be viewed primarily from a car, in this case from the A593, just north of Coniston, looking west to the Yewdale Fells. There is nowhere safe to pull off the road at the best viewpoints, so from a car White Lady is for passengers only.

WHITE LADY
making a summer appearance

# WHITE LADY

White Lady is unusual in being a totally erratic fall, which depends on the amount of rain and the saturation of the ground as to whether it flows or not. In the ideal wet conditions a long "tail" of a fall, about 25 metres (80 feet), streams over the Yewdale Fells between Mart Crag and Yewdale Crag, creating a fine spectacle. However, at other times the fall is little more than a glisten on the rocks, and occasionally nothing at all. In cold winters the rock can become a sheet of ice.

Yew Tree Farm, Yewdale

View over Yewdale on a dry summer's day

## How to get there
Grid Ref: SD 325 999
It is possible to approach this delightful little series of falls from two directions, either from Tarn Hows or from the A593 Ambleside to Coniston road.
Access Tarn Hows either from the Coniston-Hawkshead road (B5285), or from the Ambleside-Hawkshead road (B5286). Park in the lower car park at the south end of the tarn, (Grid Ref SD 325 996), free to National Trust members. Tom Gill is the small beck leaving at the southwest corner of Tarn Hows, flowing briskly down to Yewdale. The main Tom Gill fall is about 400 metres down the rocky path which follows the right side of the beck. To approach from the A593 (Coniston to Ambleside) road, park in the small National Trust car park at SD 322 999, and follow the path uphill through the woods.

TOM GILL

# TOM GILL

Visiting on a day when many of the bigger becks were in spate, and many of the falls and cascades were positively threatening, the author found the modest flow of Tom Gill a delight, especially for children. Tarn Hows has a very small catchment area and never produces the massive flows of streams and rivers draining an entire valley. There are several cascades, with the largest fall descending over an almost vertical rock slab into a shallow plunge pool. For supervised children this is perhaps the only waterfall in this book where it is possible to safely splash in the plunge pool right under the falling water.

Make Tom Gill part of a family day out. There is an ice-cream van in the car park during the season, a National Trust information van, and there are civilised toilets. Tarn Hows, though often busy, is a lovely place for a picnic and a paddle.

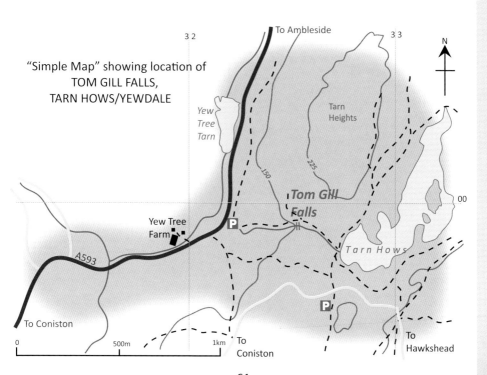

"Simple Map" showing location of
TOM GILL FALLS,
TARN HOWS/YEWDALE

32

To Ambleside

33

N

Yew Tree Tarn

Tarn Heights

150

225

Tom Gill Falls

00

Yew Tree Farm

P

Tarn Hows

A593

P

To Coniston

0    500m    1km

To Coniston

To Hawkshead

61

# FORCE FALLS

## How to get there

Grid Ref: from SD 340 911 to 337 913
Distance: 100-300 metres depending on parking. Allow 30 minutes or so.

There is not much parking in Force Mill, but you can park opposite Force Mill Guest House without blocking the road. Walk up the road towards Satterthwaite, and immediately beyond the houses, there are several access points to the Grizedale Beck as it tumbles down towards Force Forge, starting at an old metal kissing gate. The falls continue upstream for about 300 metres as far as the Bowkerstead bridge.

Alternatively, park at the picnic site 300 metres northeast of the Force Mills junction and walk down through the forest.

# FORCE FALLS

This is a delightful little section of small cascades over a few hundred metres. We visited it on a day when many other becks and rivers, including the Brathay and the Rothay were in spate, producing foaming torrents. But the Grizedale beck was just full enough to produce lovely cascades, more or less all of which were fairly safe, and highly visitable for supervised children.

As with scores of Lake District becks, the drop on the stream, at Force Mill and beyond, was used during the last few centuries, to power a variety of mills. In southern Lakeland especially, a combination of coppiced oak trees and water-powered mills, produced the bobbins which were used in the textile industries of Lancashire and Yorkshire.

One of the cascades of Force Falls

"Simple Map" showing location of
FORCE FALLS,
GRIZEDALE FOREST

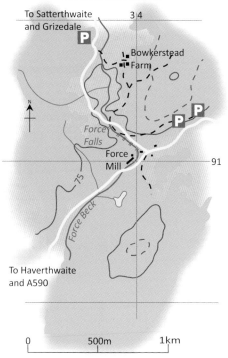

To Satterthwaite and Grizedale
3 4
Bowkerstead Farm
Force Falls
Force Mill
91
To Haverthwaite and A590
0   500m   1km

Traditional building at Force Mill

# ACKNOWLEDGEMENTS

All the Simple Maps in this book are based on data obtained and used with permission from Harvey's Lake District Outdoor Atlas, by far the most convenient single map product covering the whole of the National Park.

All the photographs in the book were taken by David and Rosemary Watson, with the exception of Taylor Force (page 20) and Stanley Gill (pages 6, 44), which were taken by David Ross, Britain Express.
(See David Ross/www.britainexpress.com)

SUGGESTIONS FOR FURTHER READING

*Exploring Lakeland Waterfalls* by Don Blair 2002

*Naturalist's Guide to Lakeland Waterfalls throughout the year* by Mary Welsh Books 1 -4. May be out of print. Obtainable in second-hand bookshops.

Many web-sites cover a selection of falls, often as part of more extensive walks. For example:
www.visitcumbria.co/force.htm
www.britainexpress.com/counties/waterfalls